High praise for *Noble Listening* ...[1]

"A true treasure! When we shift our attention toward listening, our whole world changes. Learning to listen is equal to learning to love. This creative handbook teaches us that learning to listen does not have to be a mystery. Rather, there are tangible ways that we can deepen our capacity for empathy and presence - transforming our relationships with others and ourselves. It has helped me to be a better educator, spouse, and parent. *Noble Listening* is a rare gift indeed!"

~ Ruth Cox, PhD
Institute for Holistic Healing Studies
San Francisco State University

"*Noble Listening* is a delight. It is simple, direct and profound; easy to read and follow. People crave attention and understanding, and this book will help those in all relationships improve their ability to connect, listen and love."

~ Frederic Luskin, PhD
Forgive for Good
Director, Stanford Forgiveness Project

"This delightful little book contains huge treasures, the ones that can bring us back into the joy of being human together. I imagine that if a reader only focused on two or three of the many skills given here, that they would quickly become skilled in listening, and would fall in love with the places that real conversation always takes us."
~ Margaret J. Wheatley
Leadership and the New Science

"Listening is no small skill, and so this little book is no small matter. Everyone who wants better relationships and more productivity should read this. It's fun, easy to read and speaks to the heart of the matter. I think it's a winner." ~ Richard Carlson, PhD
Don't Sweat the Small Stuff

"The foundation of good teaching is the ability to listen. Although Mark Brady writes for a much broader audience, he has provided an indispensable tool – actually, a great gift – for classroom instructors. I will carry *Noble Listening* in my pocket on a daily basis."
~ Mary Fainsod Katzenstein, PhD
Government Department
Cornell University

"This book may be little, but the significance of its message is big…very big. With appealing modesty and great sensitivity, Mark Brady offers the reader a wealth of practical tips for how to listen more attentively and effectively to others. If only a fraction of this wise advice could be put into practice, the benefits – for listener and speaker alike – would be enormous."

~ Doug McAdam, PhD
former director, Stanford Center for
Advanced Study in the Behavioral Sciences
Dynamics of Contention

"Reading *Noble Listening* should be required for all human beings, as soon as they can read and as long as their eyesight allows. The fundamentals of listening, articulated so clearly, spell out how to achieve this distinctly human skill. Don't pass up the opportunity to deepen your skill, regardless of your current level of proficiency. We can all become deeper, stronger and better listeners."

~ Joan C. King, PhD
Cellular Wisdom

"When you do what I do for a living, it's rare to find a book that's practical, satisfying, learnable and inspirational all in the same breath. *Noble Listening* is all that and much, much more. Two copies should be issued simultaneously with every marriage license."

~ Peter Pearson, PhD
In Quest of the Mythical Mate
The Couples Institute

Fierce Listening

Advanced teachings for deepening practice

by
Mark Brady, PhD

Paideia* Press
Langley, Washington

Paideia Press
P.O. Box 1294
Langley, WA 98260
(206) 201-2212
paideia@gmail.com

Copyright 2015 by Mark Brady
All Rights Reserved.

***PAIDEIA** (pie-day-a) from the Greek pais, paidos:
        lifelong learning that pays special attention
    to the spirit, heart or essence of things.

No part of this book may be reproduced in any form or by any means, including photography, recording or by information retrieval or storage systems or technologies now known or later developed, without written permission.

Library of Congress Cataloging-in-Publication Data

Brady, Mark, PhD
Fierce Listening / Mark Brady   p. cm.

ISBN -10 1505470587
ISBN -13 9781505470581

153.7'7–dc27

                                      2015111946
20 19 18 17 16 15
  6   5   4   3   2   1

Designed by Rosework Studios/Muriel Hastings
The Boy Who Finally Listened included under the educational provision of the Fair Use Doctrine

Printed in the United States of America

A POEM

My Mind and Body
    had a conversation last night
My Body said:
    Isn't it about the time for me to speak?
My Mind was surprised to hear
    that Body wanted to speak
    because, Mind was so used to speaking,
    talking, chatting,
    but... forgot
Listening.

My Body said again:
    I have my stories
    I have my language
    I have every cell to tell those stories
    I lived and died
    every day, every moment.
I remember every moment of joy
    every moment of happiness
I remember every goodbye and tear
    every sorrow and death
It is my turn to speak
My Body said it again: ... Listen

    ... because I have many stories to tell.

~ Yukari Kunisue

Why Listening? ...

Pastoral counseling professor David Augsburger has observed that "listening is the only believable sign of an open heart." Why is an open heart important? I consider that a fair question and most likely each of us will be best served to come up with our own answers, ideally by quieting our own discursive mind and then paying attention to the center of our chest and noticing any small quiverings that stir there. And then noticing the thoughts and feelings those stirrings might trigger as they generate a Somatic Narrative.

Until we actually witness the transformative effects of Fierce Listening firsthand, it's hard to believe in and trust its power. Much of what you'll find in the pages that follow are the result me my doing this kind of listening in a variety of venues for over 30 years. My interest in listening developed over several decades, primarily as I worked with grieving children. As you might expect, I discovered many things during that work - both expected and unexpected.

One thing that struck me early on in working with kids was the profound power that seemed to reside in ... mother's voice. Children who visited our agency seemed to be super-sensitively attuned to everything about mother's voice - its pitch, timbre, cadence, loudness ...

Inspired by this work and by this observation, I took to the research literature. One volume that was particularly helpful was a French ear, nose and throat doctor's book, *The Conscious Ear*. In that book, Alfred Tomatis cited research that suggested it was sensory experience in utero, minimal though it was, that drove early neural development. And of all the senses that unfolded and drove this development in utero, hearing was responsible for the majority of the early network growth and connectivity.

Tomatis argued further that it was mother's voice that was far and away the primary driver by simple virtue of its endless novelty and unpredictable variability. Applying his theory in practice, Tomatis developed a number of care centers that provided recordings of mother's voice to be sent along with children given up for adoption. When mother was not available, or a recording of her voice could not be made, Tomatis substituted Gregorian Chant to similar beneficial effect.

The key ingredient for brain development in these infants seemed to be mother's voice or the music's ability to calm and modulate states of arousal - thus effectively regulating baby's stress hormones. As we learn from research in interpersonal neurobiology, baby's brain then co-regulates mother's stress hormones as well.

Prize-winning Stanford professor, Karl Pribram, author of *The Holographic Brain,* claims that a major purpose our brain serves is to manage stress hormones in order to prevent them from adversely affecting our biology. Any training, practices or behaviors that we can place into service to support the brain's efforts at regulation inevitably have merit and prove beneficial. In my experience, Fierce Listening practice more than qualifies as such a neuro-modulator.

So, given the great benefits that inevitably accrue to a practitioner, I invite you to improve your health and have big fun while you creatively experiment with a powerful life-affirming practice - the art and science of Fierce Listening.

Table of Contents

Introduction

"Listen for the Health of It." *Page 25*

1. Talk Less
2. Hear More of What You Hear
3. Make Listening Part of a Kaizen Practice
4. Optimize Learning by Listening
5. Maximize the Power of the Open Question
6. Make De-Confabulation Safe
7. Activate Task-Negative Networks
8. Suss Out Implicatures
9. Dissolve In-Group/Out-Group Divides
10. Promote Neural Coupling
11. Practice "Kaleidoscopic" Listening
12. Be Aware of Salience Attribution
13. Pursue the Stillness in the Deep Now

Section One Reflection Questions *Page 34*

"The boy who finally listened."   *Page 37*

14. Go Against Your Dr. Dolittle Typology
15. Remedy Proximate Separation
16. Practice Fierce Listening as Stress-Busting
17. Bear the Pareto Principle in mind
18. Help Others Cultivate Viscera Eloquence
19. Honor the Power of the Coherent Narrative
20. Be More Interested than Interesting
21. Strengthen Resonance Circuits
22. Make Room for "Slow Thinking"
23. Aid in an Ordo Amorum Focus
24. Listen for Original Gravity
25. Help Turn Timely Nescience into Prescience
26. Help Give Voice to the Unthought Known

Section Two Reflection Questions   *Page 53*

"Bearing Witness" *Page 57*

27. Facilitate Neuroception
28. Champion the Capacity for Simplexity
29. Counter the Illusion-of-Truth Effect
30. Help Transcend Implicit Egotism
31. Learn to See with Your Tongue and Hear with Your Eyes
32. Mindfully Violate Expectations
33. Counteract the Cortical Bias
34. Improve Sensory Awareness by 1%
35. Become a Safe Container for Secrets
36. Expand the Harmony Window
37. Listen with the Heart in Mind
38. Don't Let the Snake Fly the Plane
39. Recognize that You're a Pleasure to Talk To

Section Three Reflection Questions *Page 73*

"The eardrums of the heart."   *Page 77*

40. Enrich Contingent Communication
41. Listen Without Intent to Do Good
42. Practice Listening to Regulate the Body
43. Activate Your Dalai Lama Neurons
44. Listen for the Loose Brick
45. Clear Your Emotional Cache
46. Listen with the Purpose of Hacking Flow
47. Make Meaning of Silence
48. Listen to Grow the 8 Intelligences
49. Ask Quality Questions
50. Transform the Dark into the Light
51. Listen for *Momento Mori*
52. Teach and Model Fierce Listening

Section Four Reflection Questions   *Page 95*

Conclusion
    The power of practice
    The power of attunement
    The power of the sangha
The Life Events Impact History
Healing Resources
Notes and References

Introduction

I've spent almost a decade designing and teaching listening skills to graduate school students planning to become helping professionals of one sort or another. When I initially poll each class and ask them to rate their current level of listening proficiency, roughly 95% identify themselves as above average. This is the Dunning-Kruger Effect showing up shamelessly in action - statistically, only 50% of any cohort can actually be *above* average.

(Cornell psychologists, David Dunning and Justin Kruger asked a number of test subjects to rate their skill levels in grammar and logic. Those who actually scored in the 12th percentile identified themselves as belonging in the 62nd percentile, clearly not having much awareness of their own level of competence).

By the end of the ten weeks of learning about, practicing, demonstrating and designing learning experiments intended to improve listening, 95% of the students come to recognize that when it came to really being a skillful listener, in their initial assessments they didn't know what they didn't know. They were basically ignorant.

None of us effectively listens in an emotional vacuum. Each of us comes to practice in the presence of other human beings. We also come to these encounters with our own levels of emotional, biological, spiritual and intellectual development, our own personal dramas and traumas, our own growing edges. Time after time we may find that the people we engage with to help us in our listening practice are struggling with the very same issues that we ourselves may be challenged to address and resolve. A history of unresolved personal trauma can seriously hamper our ability to be fully present and deeply engaged.

Like any accomplished skill, accomplished listening takes learning. You have to discover what you don't know you don't know. After learning though, then comes practice. Like guitar or piano-playing, or basketball or soccer, if you don't continually practice, your skill level will decline.

In order to keep up with practice, most of us need to operate in a context or venue where other people are regularly available for us to lend our ears to. For many years I kept up my own practice by volunteering at a community grief counseling agency. It was there that I learned firsthand about the extraordinary power that Fierce Listening can have. In addition, I also learned just how difficult and challenging such a practice can actually be.

Here in this companion book to *Noble Listening*[1] then, are some further tools that will help you keep your practice well-honed. May the power inherent in the practice be sufficient to not only keep you deeply engaged, but prove to be a defining perspective on how you view and hold what it means to be of genuine service to others.

Mark Brady
Whidbey Island, WA
January, 2015

"Listen for the Health of It"

Who benefits from support? To find out Carolyn Schwartz and Meir Sendor at Harvard recruited nonprofessionals with multiple sclerosis and trained them in active listening. These peer supporters provided telephone support over a two-year period for fifteen minutes a month to others similarly afflicted with multiple sclerosis.

The peer supporters completed a questionnaire before beginning to provide support, and again after one and two years. The participants who received support also completed the same questionnaires at the same intervals.

Three years after they finished providing active support, the peer telephone supporters were queried about the changes they noticed over the course of their participation in the study. Those who *provided* support reported improvement than those who who *received* support! They reported improved listening skills, a stronger awareness of the existence of a higher power, increased self-acceptance, and enhanced self-confidence. Peer supporters also reported experiencing a sense of inner peace that allowed them to listen to others without judgment or interference.

Interestingly, these aspects of well-being accelerated during the second year of the study. As the supporters became more effective and more outer-directed, a shift occurred in the way they thought about themselves. Participants who received support exhibited change in a number of these areas as well, but the changes were less pronounced than those experienced by the people who *provided* the support.

The authors of the study propose that these shifts occurred because of the number of personal stories the peer supporters exchanged with the people they supported. As they heard more and more stories of other people with multiple sclerosis facing challenges, the supporters were able to disengage from their usual ways of thinking about themselves and their condition. In other words, as their focus moved from concern about themselves to concern for others, their attitudes about their own multiple sclerosis altered as well. As one supporter commented: "It's tough to get depressed when you're helping someone."

Another supporter explained the change this way: "There's a quietness when I'm talking to someone, and I'm really listening to them. I have to make an effort not to try and top them. It's gotten easier. And I can listen, and I become interested in what he's talking about. That's a change. There's a quietness in the soul because of it."

~ Dr. Carolyn Schwartz
& Rabbi Meir Sendor[2]

The Practices

1. Talk less

Once again I'm listing this as the very first practice to take on as we work to become increasingly mindful, Fierce Listeners. That said, there's quite a bit to consider as we find ourselves talking less. Because we generate speech at a much slower rate than our brains process it, the lag time leaves us with more than enough time for our minds to go awandering. We need to do something skillful in order to manage that gap.

One thing that doesn't work very well is to allow our attention to become split off. In today's world with more distractions than ever before drawing our present-moment focus to one alluring distraction after another, it becomes quite easy to "disconnect" both attentionally and emotionally. How that then shows up in a speaker's experience as your body being present, but your heart and mind are clearly elsewhere. It's like a Skype call suddenly going dark.

This difficulty with sustaining focused attention is one of the central challenges that make skillful listening so Fierce. It's also why it takes ongoing, dedicated practice. And there's no time off for good behavior.

Practice: *Notice the kinds of distractions that prove most difficult to ignore as you engage with* *others. Does a cell phone or computer tablet easily draw you away? Competing conversations? Intrusive non-relevant thoughts? The fact that our eyes so easily override our ears as sensory processors? With that noticing, keep bringing your attention back to the speaker. The more you practice, the easier it will become.*

2. Hear More of What You Hear

Former NY Yankee all-star catcher, Yogi Berra is well-known for his "Yogi-isms." One often attributed to him is, "You can hear a lot by listening." More than just a waggish tautology, it turns out that intentionally taking up a listening practice actually can work to improve our hearing.

As with anything we devote time, energy and neural resources toward becoming more skillful with, the time we devote to mindful listening can positively impact the cells and transmission fibers in the temporal lobes of our brain and in the auditory cortex.

Biophysiologist, Stephen Porges at the University of North Carolina has been researching the effects of listening on the brain for a number of years. His research lab attempts to engage the active cortical control of the middle ear muscles as a portal to the Social Engagement System. What this means is that the potential of learning to listen deeply can radically and positively affect structures in the brain in ways that are both pro-social and neurologically transformational. Essentially, by learning to hear more of what we hear, we become more engaging and enjoyable to spend time with![3]

Practice: *Pay attention to how frequently you talk over and say things that emotionally upset other people. What do you think might be motivating such behavior? If your roles were reversed, how might you prefer to be engaged with in a similar situation?*

3. Make listening part of a Kaizen practice

Kaizen is a Japanese word that literally means "good change." It can be continuous, ongoing or a one-time improvement, large or small. It refers more to a mindset than it does to any specific activity or way of being.

As a mindset where it concerns Fierce Listening, one way to practice Kaizen might simply be to begin paying attention each time we find ourselves listening less than skillfully. For example, each time we notice "our story taking over their story," or "find ourselves 'shoulding' on someone" we might simply pause and redirect our responses.

UCLA psychologist Robert Maurer, in his book, *One Small Step: The Kaizen Way*[4] suggests that small improvements in listening practice might involve things like thinking small thoughts, or identifying small moments for practice, or taking small steps to solve small problems. Over time, the accumulated collection of small, good changes can result in a very great change in our practice of Fierce Listening.

Practice: *Identify one small, good change that you might be able to make in the way you customarily listen to people. For example, you might initiate a curious inquiry if your someone who customarily waits for others to speak so that you can response. Or you might simply invite someone to deeper exploration with the invitation: "Tell me more."*

4. Practice FTD Listening

Think of a newborn baby - here's how she learns. Every new encounter, every new fact, every novel sensory experience grows a new cell or makes new connections in her brain. The neurons in her brain don't simply represent learning - they <u>are</u> the learning. This is true for all of us - young or old, newborn or septuagenarian.[5]

FTD listening makes use of this process by inviting people to Feel, Think and Do. Thinking, Feeling and Doing recruit neural networks connecting and strengthening both hemispheres of the brain as well as the body.

Now think about this: who learns more - a speaker or a listener? In order for someone to be a speaker, they most often end up speaking about things they already know, or at least think they know (confabulation is a widespread affliction all across the planet - it's the storyteller part of the brain making stuff up and then forgetting that it has). There may be some thinking, feeling and doing going on, but there's very little new learning happening while someone is expounding on this, that or the other thing.

A Fierce Listener, on the other hand, especially one with an open, curious mind whose tuned in to a speaker's feelings, actions and thoughts can actually shape and lead a conversation in directions where she is able to make new discoveries and learn new things. In other words, grow widespread new brain cells and make new connections!

Practice: *Notice how powerful listening can be for feeling, thinking and doing - for learning; practice learning one new thing in every encounter you have with the people around you.*

Ask Open Questions that invite feeling, thinking and doing.

5. Maximize the Power of the Open Question

An Open Question is essentially a vehicle for exploring the world with a curious mind. It is a way of organizing experience as a young child might - filled with wonder, inquisitiveness and nescience (See Practice 26).

Elizabeth Mattis-Namgyel, in her book, *The Power of an Open Question*[6], suggests that Open Questions tend to help us find our way through many of life's great complexities to a very simple way of sensing and being ... in the "hear" and now. Out of such questions, rooted authentically in "not-knowing," grows us out of habitual, reactive mind into an increasing ability to rivet our attention onto our own and other's experience, especially those experiences that we "don't want to talk about" or would prefer to avoid and turn away from.

The suffering in the world is widespread. It needs people with the developed capacity to turn towards it and bear compassionate witness in ways that do not contribute to further suffering. To get the feel and flavor, imagine a child innocent and open to a favorite uncle recently diagnosed and hospitalized with cancer.

Practice: *Spend a day doing your best to pay close attention to people, places and things with a sense of engaged curiosity. What do you see on your way to work that you normally overlook. How have the people you know and see regularly changed in small ways in what they believe and how they act? Type a random word into your computer's search box and see what stored files it presents to you? Who were you and what meaning did that information have when you originally stored it?*

6. Make De-Confabulation Safe

Nobody likes to come across as ignorant. Many of us will do everything we can to seem knowledgeable, intelligent and wise. That drive is actually built into our brain's language circuitry and has served us well for thousands of years. When our brain doesn't understand something, it makes up stories. That's called *confabulation*. Confabulation is essentially an "alien subroutine," one that doesn't have to be a problem. But the brain makes it into one by adding a little something extra: it makes us forget that the stories we're making up aren't true, especially in the here and now.

What's a skillful response then, when

we recognize the fact that someone's brain is making something up? Unless their confabulation poses a dangerous threat to themselves or others, is there really any great need to "set the record straight?" What might be at the root of such a need in you? Might further, curious inquiry be a gift in response when it doesn't trigger embarrassed defensiveness or big streams of stress hormones in the speaker?

Practice: *Think of a time when stressful circumstances caused your brain to make up a story and tell it to someone else. What effect did being "found out" have upon your body? Even as you recall or imagine such a time, what effect is it having upon you now?*

7. Activate Task-Negative Networks

There's a significant imbalance and bias that operates in today's world that becoming a Fierce Listener can help right. It's called "the cortical bias." Essentially, it refers to the brain's preference for thinking over feeling, and for "doing" over "being."

The "task-negative network" is the term that researchers use to describe the brain circuitry involved in daydreaming. While daydreaming is rarely highly valued or prized in many work or learning environments, Einstein recognized it as one of his most important tools when he said, "The true sign of intelligence isn't knowledge; it's imagination."

A Fierce Listener can be a champion of daydreaming and imagination by offering up "Yes, and" and "What if" responses to speaker's self-limiting, circumscribed beliefs. This freedom to daydream and explore forbidden or taboo subject areas has been shown to be beneficial by establishing and strengthening connections in the brain that might not otherwise ever become connected.[7]

Practice: Notice the number of times that your mind arbitrarily places a limitation upon what's possible for you to engage in or accomplish during any day. What might be some effective ways for you to move beyond your current manifest reality? Who might you enlist to help you move in the direction of your night dreams and your daydreams?

8. Suss Out Implicatures

British philosopher Paul Grice[8] worked for much of his life to find hidden meanings in the ordinary language we use every day. He discovered that people often mean something other than the literal meanings of the words and the syntax they use. Grice called these hidden meanings *implicatures* - people saying one thing, but implying another, often the very opposite of words they use. Furthermore, people can sometimes say what they mean, but also mean something else in addition.

This use of indirect speech can operate as a powerful social glue, allowing people to interact and cooperate without direct confrontation.

But it can also lead to a lot of misunderstandings and confusion in personal and professional relationships. Which makes it useful and important to "suss out implicatures" - that is, investigate and figure out the different or additional things when people say what they say but not all that they mean.

Practice: *Begin to pay attention to the various levels of meaning that run through many of the things that people say to each other every day. Pay particular attention to how this particular manner of using language operates as a means for regulating stress and anxiety in the course of human social interactions. Without our ability to use implicatures, what do you imagine might happen to the social contract as a result?*

9. Dissolve In-Group/Out-Group Divides

Whether we realize it or not, much of the work we do as Fierce Listeners is to help people dissolve the illusory trance of separation. Much like the cells in a working brain, human beings are part of a worldwide network called ... humanity. How we treat each other matters. It matters on the global level and it matters at the cellular level.

Neuroscientist Daniel Levitin, in his book *The Organized Mind*,[2] details the adverse impact that holding artificial in-group/out-group divisions has upon our brain. Essentially, it reduces our capacity for cognitive complexity as we recognize, hold and validate rich characteristics of people like us (our in-groups), and simplistically and stereotypically think about and characterize people different from us (our out-groups). The whole world (brain) suffers when we maintain such illusory representations.

Practice: *Begin to notice how other people- especially "foreigners" - make you nervous. Where do you mostly feel the discomfort? In your throat? Your back? Your abdomen? As a tightness in your mind? What practices might you begin to place into service that might allow* *you to skillfully address and resolve or at least reduce this tension or anxiety?*

10. Promote Neural Coupling

For as long as human beings have been able to use language, stories have played a central role, not only in our collective history, but also in the history of our evolving brain. Fierce Listeners, it turns out, by listening to the physically and emotionally rich accounts of others, benefit by what New York Times columnist, Annie Murphy-Paul describes as "rich neural coupling."[9]

In addition to the two language centers in the brain's left hemisphere (Wernicke's Area & Broca's Area), scientists have come to realize that narratives activate many other areas as well. Words like "lemon," "lilac" and "limburger," for example, elicit a response not only from the language areas of our brains, but also those devoted to dealing with smells.

When speakers use metaphors like "a rough day" or "smooth sailing," scientists at Emory University report that the sensory cortex, which perceives texture through touch, become active. Metaphors like "Mel Torme has a velvet voice" and "The sea captain has leathery hands" stimulated the sensory cortex, while phrases matched for meaning, like "Mel Torme has a pleasing voice" and "The sea captain has strong hands," did not.

Areas in the brain responsible for body movement are also neurally coupled in listener and speaker when action verbs are spoken. A study by Véronique Boulenger, of the Laboratory of Language Dynamics in France,[10] found that when the brains of participants were scanned as they read sentences like "Pierre grasped the bat" and "Pablo kicked the ball," activity in the motor cortex, which coordinates the body's movements was observed. Interestingly, this activity was concentrated in different areas when the movement described was arm-related and in another part when the movement involved the leg.

The brain, it seems, does not make much of a distinction between speaking about an experience and encountering it in real life; in each case, the relevant neurological regions are stimulated.

Practice: *Spend some time during the coming week noticing how spoken words rich in descriptive language actually impact and resonate in your body. Can you increasingly distinguish between subtle expressions of taste, smell or touch? Where in your body do you feel most affected by strong language?*

11. Practice "Kaleidoscopic" Listening

Fierce Listening involves more than just our ears and their connections to our brain. Nor does it take place in a social, emotional or intellectual vacuum. Among many other aspects, has biological, chemical, neurological, psychological, medical, emotional, social, political, economic and spiritual underpinnings.

To deepen practice, we can become versed in many of these areas as well as others. By continuing to turn and view the kaleidoscope that make up so many diverse areas of human experience, we increase the possibility of a deep connection with ourselves and others, along with an expanding capacity to see a much more complete picture. Similar to the auto mechanic who can listen to an engine and tap a spark plug wire with a screwdriver handle and cure rough running, so too can a Fierce Listener bring a life of kaleidoscopic experience to bear.

Practice: *Give some thought to other areas that can positively impact on listening that I haven't mentioned here. One example that comes immediately to mind: the context or environment where listening takes place.*

12. Be Aware of Salience Attribution

Many of the things that people often talk about with great sincerity and considerable intensity, and that we end up listening to at great length, turn out to actually be animated expressions of false needs. To continue to give more time and energy to such expressions often proves less than useful. Pema Chodron identifies such instances a "idiot listening." In the field of addiction research the tendency to assign great value to false needs at the expense of true needs is called "salience attribution."

TED talker, Hospice chaplain and cancer "experiencer," Debra Jarvis talks of the requirement to confront cancer "survivors." Whenever she encounters someone overly invested in their identity as a survivor, she makes it a point when they express feeling crucified, to invite them to come down from their cross. Whatever benefits they may be receiving as a "survivor" need to be traded up for something richer: authentic living in the present moment.[11]

One Fierce way to stop Idiot Listening and cut through salience attribution is to simply ask the question: "What are you most needing right now." Invariably, such a question pulls a speaker up short, causing them to pause and reflect. This momentary pause and reflection often makes room for real, deeper needs to emerge.

Practice: *Find a half dozen opportunities to practice asking the question, "What are you most needing right now?" this week. See what kinds of responses come back to you in response to this invitation to depth and authenticity.*

13. Pursue the Stillness in the Deep Now

There's a powerful and diabolical illusion that affects many of us in the day-to-day living of our lives. It's this - that we can do more than one thing at a time with little energy expenditure or loss of effectiveness.

But Willie Loman (Death of a Salesman) was right: Not only must attention be paid, but paying attention has a cost. We pay for it by using energy - electro-chemical firings in the brain. When we think we're multi-tasking effectively, what we're actually doing is switching from one task to another very rapidly. This expends much more brain energy than a singular focus does.

Fierce Listeners conserve energy. They devote their whole attention to listening fully with as few distractions as possible. In his book, *The Rise of Superman*, neurobiologist Stephen

Kotler[12] describes the "hypo-frontality" that arises as an altered state of consciousness. He describes that state as "The Deep Now." In Deep Now states, very little energy is used by the prefrontal cortex, the part of the brain where higher cognitive functions reside, along with our sense of morality, our sense of will, and our sense of self. What Kotler is essentially describing is ... the timeless practice of presence.

Practice: *Notice the amount of time in any day when we find ourselves attempting to do more than one thing at a time. What is driving this need for distraction? If you were to design a personal practice intended to skillfully address this tendency in yourself, what might that actually look and feel like?*

Section One Reflection Questions

Of these first 13 skills, which stand out the most as I practice to become a skilled listener?

What have I heard that I haven't been able to hear before I began practicing these skills?

I am working to create an atmosphere of trust by...

Notes to myself...

*"Since, in order to speak, one must first hear,
do you come to speech by way of hearing?"*
~ Rumi

The Boy Who Finally Listened

Once upon a time there was a boy who had stopped listening. So his ears grew smaller and smaller until at last finally they disappeared. And so, naturally, no one ever thought to tell him a story. And though his head was filled with pictures of the world, and he raced here and there to do a million things, there was something missing. He could not find a home for his imagination. And the beautiful box of wonder in his mind remained always just out of reach.

Then one day he came upon a storyteller telling stories to children in the park. His eyes sparkled, and he wore a raggedy suit with all the colors of the earth and sky. With his deep gentle voice he wove a wondrous tapestry for the children gathered at his feet. And as he spoke, a miracle occurred - two tiny ears, no bigger than a freckle, appeared on either side of the boy's head, and for the very first time ... he began to listen.

The boy returned to the park every day, and with each story his ears grew eagerly. They grew and grew. Until one day the boy's ears opened like doors. And the music of the world became a symphony.

~ Alan Scofield

14. Go Against Your Dr. Dolittle Typology

Professor Kimberly Batty-Herbert[13] has done research that suggests that many of us conform to a listening style or type that correlates with a number of the animals from the Dr. Dolittle books. Here are her characterizations:

Bull - stubborn, self-centered, defensive
Gorilla - attacks when confronted
Koala - passive, quiet
Buffalo - appears aloof,
    but can charge at any time
Snake - slithers around, untrustworthy,
    ambushes
Turkey - oddball, unorganized, feathers
    are easily ruffled
Owl - wise, intelligent, always prepared to
    give you his or her opinion or
    advice, highly critical
Lion - king of the jungle; always needs to
    be in charge
Kangaroo - jumps around; can't predict
    where they are headed or what
    subject to focus on
Monkey - out for a good time; rarely
    serious

Turtle - slow, hard to get them motivated; goes into their shell when uncomfortable or feeling threatened
Parrot - continually repeats what you say; rarely expresses original thoughts
Peacock - constantly struts his stuff; egotistical; stage-hogger
Ostrich - sticks its head in the sand, avoids subjects they don't want to hear about, insulates self from disturbing topics

Practice: *Do any of these animals and their listening styles resonate with your natural inclinations? If you were to go against your own type, which ones might you most easily adopt? Which ones might prove most challenging for you? Are those the ones that you might benefit most from trying on?*

15. Remedy Proximate Separation

The proliferation of cell phones, tablets, electronic readers and other electronic devices provides great benefits, but they also come with a downside. One downside is observable instances of what addiction specialist Gabor Mate calls "proximate separation."[14]

Proximate separation can be observed in every mall, every playground and virtually every social venue in the world: two or more people in close enough proximity to be able to carry on a conversation. Instead, they are each glued to one sort of electronic device or another.

This lack of attuned, direct interpersonal exchange is having a profoundly negative impact on the brains of children and young adults. Such engagement is essential for growing and strengthening the "resonance circuits" in the brain, as well as the circuitry needed for emotional self-regulation in face-to-face exchanges with others. Without that circuitry, forming strong, lasting, committed relationships becomes a considerable challenge.

Practice: *Next time you're at the mall or at any public event, spend time noticing just how many people standing or sitting in close proximity are busy with their heads buried in an electronic device. What might you do to get them to change that behavior that doesn't have a high probability of triggering a defensive reaction?*

16. Practice Fierce Listening as Stress-Busting

Stanford neurobiologist, Robert Sapolsky [15] has studied stress for a significant part of his academic career. He's identified four conditions that almost always increase our stress hormones to damaging levels.

The first condition is walking through the world and feeling we have very little control over our lives. This is a common experience many adults have in their work lives. It's also the predominant experience children have, often on into early adulthood. Feeling like we have little control in our lives turns out to be very stressful.

The second major source of stress in our lives is being required to live with little predictability. Going day after day with little structure or certainty or predictability elevates stress levels. These high levels invariably take a toll on our body and brain.

The third greatly impactful stressor turns out to be living a day-to-day life with little social support. We need other people in our lives for all kinds of reasons, stress management being one of the most important.

Fourth and finally, without sufficient awareness of the stressors in our live and multiple creative outlets for skillfully managing them, we are almost certain to unwittingly ratchet up our stress to unhealthy levels

A Fierce Listener can be an essential ally in helping other people both identify the stressors in their lives, which often operate outside conscious awareness, and in finding creative ways to effectively address them.

Practice: *How do you know when you yourself feel especially stressed? Some people only know their stress levels are way high when they get sick or have an accident, or make some other serious mistake. One person confessed that only when she gets a traffic ticket does she discover that her stress levels are out of control. If you can begin to recognize your own tell-tale somatic signs that your stress loads are at unhealthy levels, you'll be more readily able to help others recognize and address their stress.*

17. Bear the Pareto Principle in mind

The Pareto Principle is better known as the 80-20 Rule. What it means in terms of Fierce Listening is that only a small portion of what you hear will take you deeper into areas that have great heart and meaning for the speaker. But your job isn't to immediately dismiss all the great deal of expression that often needs to precede a speaker's ability to find her way to great depths. Your job is to listen attentively with great curiosity to both the content and the process of the speaker. And to do this with great patience. What many listeners eventually come to find is that much of the work of Fierce Listening is primarily the work of strengthening a "patience practice."

Practice: *Notice the next time you're engaging with someone and the impulse or desire arises in you where you wish they would "get on with it." Or "get to the point, already." What might you be able to do in order to simply observe that impulse in yourself and not need to speak to it or address it overtly with the speaker?*

18. Help Others Cultivate Viscera Eloquence

The viscera make up all the hollow organs in the human body. Each of these organs is tied to the brain by the 10th cranial (vagus) nerve. The distributed energy and information network that is essentially how our operates is constantly transmitting, but mostly receiving information day in and day out from our viscera.

In her book, *Body Eloquence*, psychotherapist Nancy Mellon[16] argues that it's possible to actually attend to and learn the subtle energy patterns and "language" that our viscera use to communicate to our brain with. Fierce Listeners first work to understand the deep wisdom of their own hollow organ transmissions and then work to help others come to apprehend and trust their own hard-won viscera-wisdom.

Practice: *Learn the names of and the location of the hollow organs in your body. The stomach, for example, is not located in the belly as many people believe, but rather, is located on the left side just below the heart, which is actually closer to the centerline of the body than most people realize. As you learn the names and locations of these organs - for example, the adrenal glands sitting atop your kidneys - begin to pay attention and learn the way each of these organs expresses themselves in healthy operation.*

19. Honor the Power of the Coherent Narrative

Fierce Listeners readily recognize when the things people say don't make sense. They also attend closely to unintended or accidental displays of emotion. Each is a sign that a speaker is struggling to express what psychologists call a "coherent narrative." Coherent narratives help us make sense and meaning of our lives. Things like betrayal, abandonment and abusive trauma can work to undermine the ability for clear sense and meaning-making.

Elaine Reese[17] and her colleagues have done extensive research which shows that being able to express a coherent narrative highly correlates with accurate memory, self-understanding, better physical and psychological health and closer family relationships.

Bearing this developmental health requirement in mind, Fierce Listeners learn to appreciate and welcome confusion and emotional expression in others. By being able to bear compassionate witness they afford the possibility of helping another regain and restore a sense of meaning and value to their lives and the suffering they have managed to endure. A speaker's life can once again return to being something that "makes sense."

Practice: *Notice the next time you hear someone interrupt a conversation with a distracting non-sequitur. Or when some speaks and the things they say sound scattered or fragmented. Finally, notice and pay close attention to what goes on in you when someone expresses strong emotions, either sadness, uncontrollable joy or great anger. How do you generally respond to such expression? How would you ideally like to respond?*

20. Be More Interested than Interesting

Don't just *act* interested; *be* interested. Be curious. Think of interactions with people as treasure hunts. Everyone you meet holds great deposits of vast riches. Your mission, should you choose to grow your Fierce Listening brain and heart cells, is to see if you can uncover the Mother Lode. Not in yourself so that you can feel free to impress people with all you've accomplished and how great you are, but rather as a way to help facilitate another's growth and development.

But what if you're simply not interested in a person and what they have to say? Well, you might want to consider that you may be suffering from a "failure of imagination." You can find something interesting about even the most boring, self-absorbed person on the planet. For example, you might be curious about how she or he got that way? What are the (fearful?) things that currently keep them so dull? What things in their lives do they feel require them to be courageous and take risks?

Practice: *Think of the most boring person in your personal or professional circle. Make time to spend with that person. Use that time for* *practice discovering creative ways to be in relationship with people who put you to sleep. What helps that practice? What hinders it? Might that person simply be a reflection of this wisdom teaching: "We do not see people as they are; we see them as we are."*

21. Strengthen Brain Resonance Circuits

As the brain develops in us as children, every person , place or thing that we come in contact with either gets represented by new cells, or by new connections between existing cells. If we've had parents sufficiently enlightened such that we got to spend a lot of time around a wide diversity of other kids, then we developed circuitry in our brain that began to make those kids feel very familiar to us. Upon meeting these kids or other kids who reminded us of earlier ones, the circuitry in the brain that begins firing neuroscientists call "resonance circuits."

I number of neuroscientists at UCLA[18] have proposed that mirror neurons make up part of the brain's resonance circuitry. Mirror neurons were literally discovered by "monkey see, monkey do." When a lab researcher[19] ate a banana, corresponding neurons in a monkey's brain began firing. This circuitry is also responsible for our direct experience of empathy.

Fierce Listeners are afforded a great opportunity to both strengthen the resonance circuitry in their own brains, and the resonance circuitry in a multitude of speakers brains by the simple act of Fierce Listening.

Practice: *Spend some time practicing making the distinction between" thinking about" a feeling someone may be experiencing and actually feeling the feeling someone else may be having. If it's too difficult to begin with people initially, you might want to practice at first with a pet.*

22. Make Room for "Slow Thinking"

In 2002 psychologist Daniel Kahneman shared the Nobel Prize in, of all things, economics. It was for his research that proved - human beings are not rational creatures.

Extending that work, Kahneman wrote a book entitled, *Thinking Fast and Slow*. Fast Thinking tends to be immediate, reactive and often driven by our neurophysiology. Slow Thinking on the other hand often comes later and is more considered, more deliberate, more responsive and uses very different parts of the brain.[20]

Fierce Listeners understand that "first though, best thought" may not be the whole truth and nothing but. They recognize that human beings are enormously complex and that tender memories and connections stored in the body and brain may need some time and space to safely emerge. They make time and space for such possibilities to surface.

Practice: *Notice the times over the next few days when your reactive mind is urging you to take some kind of action in the world. What steps are you able to take to successfully abstain? What deeper needs or insights might your own reactive mind be attempting to direct you toward?*

23. Aid in an Ordo Amorum Focus

Saint Augustine was a Catholic bishop, the patron saint of brewers, printers and theologians. Realizing in the 4th century AD that he was suffering from information overload, Augustine came up with the concept of the *ordo amorum*, which is Latin for "the ordering of our loves." As the poet, Wendell Berry has pointed out, some loves are greater than others and lay greater claim on our lives. Nevertheless, for many of us a strong need can arise that directs us to make the often difficult decisions involved in choosing between what we love over what we love most.

Fierce Listeners, by being aware that often the difficulties that permeate people's lives are often aware of this very *ordo amorum* nature - the forced need to make hard choices between what we love and what we love most. Pain is often involved in such choices and to the extent a Fierce Listener can be fully present and not distract or turn away from the attendant pain, they perform great, beneficial service.

Practice: *Give some thought to what ideally has "great heart and meaning" in your own life. How did those people, places and things come to have that meaning? What do you actually need to do in order to keep them in the forefront of daily awareness? Is there someone who might be able to help you in this endeavor? Are there external time and place structures (like a daily calendar reminder) that can support you in this practice?*

24. Listen for Original Gravity

Original Gravity is the euphemism that brewers in Great Britain use to measure "the mystery of beer," to somehow assess its depth and essence. The stronger the Original Gravity, the deeper and more mysterious the resulting brew.

Fierce Listeners can apply this metaphor as a lens through which to take in speakers at increasing levels of depth and mystery. We all are, after all, great works in progress. Who we are, who we're becoming and who we'll be is essentially unpredictable at the level of worldly life. But Fierce Listening holds the potential to work magic in strengthening and deepening Original Gravity in both speaker and listener.

Practice: *Consider that most every person you encounter is on a journey of growth and development. What might they be yearning to express and discover that could move them on to the next leg of that journey, whatever it may be? How might you as a Fierce Listener best facilitate it?*

25. Help Turn Timely Nescience into Prescience

Prescience is the ability to unconsciously or intuitively come to gain foreknowledge about the future. Nescience is not exactly the opposite and it's more complicated than simple ignorance. While related to "not knowing," nescience can also refer to an unknown unknown - something that no human being can never begin to imagine knowing.

There are great realms of ignorance that your dog can't even imagine, much less learn about and thus rid itself of that ignorance. That's another, more esoteric definition of nescience

Neuroscientists and psychologists claim that many of us have a dishonest, complicated relationship with nescience, and it's that lying that we do to ourselves which keeps us sane and happy.

Fierce Listeners have a clear understanding that shining the light of awareness on nescience is often a dicey proposition requiring proper season and seasoning along with kindness and "big picture" awareness.

Practice: *How do you assess whether or not someone is ready to have you reflect back hard truths to them? To point out things that might be obvious to others, but blind to them? How might you determine when it's the right time for the blind to begin to see?*

26. Help Reveal the Unthought Known

Much that drives our daily life does so at an unconscious level. The brain makes note of and records experiences long before we take our first breath. It also does so after that first breath, and continues to do so up until around 18 months, when the structures in the brain are primed to learn language. Every important (i.e. scary) experience that we learned about in utero and before language is stored , often as body sensations in something called implicit memory. English psychiatrist Christopher Bolas[21] has given the unconscious learning that we acquire during this time before language the name, The Unthought Known.

The Unthought Known - different than the Unknown Unknown from the previous practice - is difficult to access. It needs time and the feeling of safety and a context within which that work is being taken seriously. It also can require a speaker to show up psychologically. energetically and emotionally as very young and vulnerable, especially if memories of early trauma live there.

Part of the gift a Fierce Listener can provide is an understanding of and a willingness to be present to the emotional reality of The Unthought Known. By affording a person the opportunity to speak in depth at length about this period of their lives, the brain can begin to make sense of thoughts and feelings that might not make sense otherwise. A sense of calm and hope is often the result as a speaker is gradually able to formulate a "coherent narrative." A coherent narrative – being able to speak clearly about early life events without becoming emotionally upset – is one indicator that a traumatic experience has been fully worked through.

***Practice:** If people who were around who were present at your birth (or before), or in the first two years of your life, interview them and see what they might recall of early experiences that might have adversely impacted you. Can you make a connection from those experiences to things you either gravitate toward or turn away from in your current life?*

Section Two Reflection Questions

What changes have I noticed in my relationships since I've begun practicing these listening skills?

What conflicts have I been able to resolve since I've been practicing these skills?

What things am I newly curious about or interested in about other people?

Notes to myself...

"I have finally become aware that those who listen are usually the ones whose wisdom trumps information."
~ Allan Ross Hicks

"Bearing Witness"

A few years ago, I was introduced to the practice of "bearing witness." This is not a religious practice. Rather, it's a simple practice of being brave enough to sit with human suffering, to acknowledge it for what it is, to not flee from it. It doesn't make the suffering go away, although it sometimes changes the experience of pain and grief. When I bear witness, I turn toward another and am willing to let their experience enter my heart.

We are living in a time of increased human suffering. There is still great poverty, growing hunger, more devastation from disease. There is more warfare, more people on the move seeking refuge in temporary camps. More people devastated by natural disasters of famine, flood, storms, earthquakes.

How we respond to so much suffering is our choice. We can feel hopeless and overwhelmed by this world; we can turn away and just live the best life we can. Or we can learn to bear witness. Sometimes I take whatever photo of recent devastation is available from the newspaper - a mother in a refugee camp, a child of war, a family crouched in a shelter - and I just gaze into it, making eye contact, trying to keep my heart open. It's a simple way to keep myself from fleeing from their experience. I can't do much to help, but at least I can link eyes with them, and bear witness to their sorrow. I don't do this to feel better. I do this to keep myself from hiding from the reality of other people's lives.

I've tried other ways to bear witness. Standing and patiently listening to someone I'd rather avoid. Or consciously reading stories of tragedy, torture, massacres - instead of changing channels or turning past the page in a magazine. I used to feel that these horrors were just too much for me to bear. But now I'm learning to read through to the end by reminding myself that I have a role here. If people have survived such atrocities, I honor them by reading about their experiences. They lived it; the least I can do is read about it.

If the world were going smoothly, if life were growing easier, it wouldn't matter so much which way we were turning. But most of us feel that the world is deteriorating, and we don't expect it to be improving any time soon. Because this is a difficult time for so many, we need a better way to be with hardships and devastation. We can turn away, or we can turn toward. Those are the only two choices we have.

~Margaret Wheatley
Turning Toward One Another

27. Facilitate Neuroception

Our brain is essentially a network that distributes energy and information. One of the places it distributes that energy and information is back and forth to our body. More specifically, it distributes it to our *viscera* - our hollow organs.

The hollow organs, it turns out, have a language they speak. It's one our brain is continually listening to; and it's a language we can all learn. To learn that language, first it's useful to understand a process called *neuroception*. Neuroception is a process originated by biophysiologist Stephen Porges [22] based on his research into Polyvagal Theory - how the twin vagus nerve bundles that weave all through our body, essentially run our lives outside our awareness.

Porges defines neuroception as "threat detection without awareness." It's the "without awareness" part that Fierce Listeners have a great opportunity to be significantly impactful with. Why? Because the fears that many of us walk around with day in and day out are mostly the result of body sending secret fearful message to our brain without CCing the conscious part of us during the transmission. Fierce Listeners then, can provide the great gift of making the unconscious threats that limit our lives, more conscious. When we know what we're afraid of, it begins to lose it's power over us.

Practice: *List a dozen ways that your life feels circumscribed by things you "can't quite put your finger on." For example, you might think that you're earning less livelihood than you feel you could. Or you may identify limits to intimacy in your own life and the lives of those around you. As you list these things, pay particular attention to sensations that arise in your body.*

28. Champion the Capacity for Simplexity

We all have worlds within us that we haven't even begun to open the doors to. The brain's and body's very organization is a study in enormous complexity. Much of our work as Fierce Listeners however, is often to take that complexity and whittle and edit it down to its simplest essence, but nothing less. For ourselves, and for other people.

A common example is Auguste Rodin's description of his statue-creation process: "I choose a block of marble and chop off whatever I don't need."

This process of taking the complex and pruning it to its simplest essence and nothing less I call *simplexity*. Simplexity turns out to a practice that can be cultivated, one that, with practice, becomes a joyful and ecstatic way to walk through the world.

Practice: *Look around your office or living space. What might you do to bring to the complexity you very likely discover there? Are there things you could do without? Things that you would feel more spaciousness and serenity to have a place for and to have what needs to be in it, in it?*

29. Counter the Illusion-of-Truth Effect

The brain uses two kinds of memory - explicit and implicit. Explicit memory allows for conscious recall. Not so much with implicit. Explicit memory can forget things. Rarely does implicit. The Illusion-of-Truth Effect operates on this fundamental feature of human memory. How it works is if we have seen or heard something before, even if we don't recall it, we are more likely to believe it's true.

Fierce Listeners realize that many things paired together in time and space, the brain tends to later associate together, creating the feeling of familiarity, and thus of truth. Just because a speaker swears an experience or event is true - and they may honestly and emotionally believe it

\- doesn't necessarily mean that it is. As viewing a skillful magician will fully attest, our senses are not always to be completely trusted.

Practice: *Spend some time paying attention to print and video advertisements. Notice how ads tend to pair things together in order to get you to make pleasant associations that will hopefully lead to a sale. What do you need to do to not be overly influenced by such pairings? By the "truth" in advertising?*

30. Help Transcend Implicit Egotism

People tend to be drawn to others who reflect their own positive qualities (including even having names that begin with the same letter![23]). Psychologists call this self-love or *implicit egotism*.

As you might suspect, Implicit Egotism works against diversity, promotes in-group versus out-group conflict and contributes to much suffering in the world.

One primary challenge with helping people transcend Implicit Egotism is that it generally operates out of implicit memory - people are unaware of the fact that these unconscious influences are running operations as much as they are. How to skillfully bring them to the point of conscious awareness is high level work in Fierce Listening.

Practice: *Do a Google search on "cognitive biases." Take a look at how many ways we operate unconsciously and rarely realize it. Which of these biases do you recognize in yourself? How many do you think might be operating without you having any awareness of them at all?*

31. Learn to See with Your Tongue and Hear with Your Eyes

There are many recorded observations in neuroscience that demonstrate the fact that one sense can indeed substitute for another. Some people, like synesthetes, appear to come pre-wired that way. But Baylor University professor David Eagleman[24] has clearly demonstrated our capacity for using our sense of touch to facilitate hearing in the deaf, essentially proving that sense substitution is a learnable skill (which we've long known from how neurons in the visual cortex of the blind get recruited and deployed into service in the use of a cane and in reading braille).

Can we actually learn to see with our tongues and hear with our eyes? We can't definitively say "No," and in fact, Eric Weihenmayer was the first blind person to climb Mount Everest. He did it with a "Brainport," a chip with 600 tiny electrodes attached to his tongue that ran to his visual cortex.

We can use this possibility and all kinds of other sense substitutions as a metaphor to help speakers entertain and explore all kinds of creative options that they may never have considered in attempting to deal with the challenging circumstances of their lives.

Practice: *Begin exploring the possibility of learning to* sense-substitute *on your own. What colors might your favorite kinds of music look like? Or what might some of the most popular YouTube videos (Gangnam Style?) taste like?*

32. Mindfully Violate Expectations

Much of our brain operates on what brain scientists call "zombie systems." Things happen automatically without us paying much attention to them. We get up, wash, brush our teeth, go to work, etc. Much of it happens on automatic pilot.

Fierce Listeners, though, practice becoming skillful at useful pattern interruptions, at violating expectations, usually for the benefit of the speaker. They often say and do things that a speaker might not expect (like listening closely for an extended amount of time without interrupting; or listening with a full focus!). One benefit violating expectations often provides is an increase in cognitive flexibility for both the listener and speaker.

Practice: Next time you're in an exchange with another person, listen for any slight quivery impulses that may spontaneously arise inviting you to respond in a way that feels either a lot or a little "out of character." What would it take for you to become comfortable in having these impulses arrive on a regular basis and for you to confidently act on them?

33. Counteract the Cortical Bias

Much of the current education that takes place in the world is focused on STEM subjects - Science, Technology, Engineering and Math. These subjects generally represent what neurophysiologist Stephen Porges[22] has termed "the cortical bias." These subjects are mostly studied by men and they mostly involve the workings of the left cortical hemisphere.

One challenge is that such an education creates imbalanced cortical connections in the human brain. That imbalance then extends to the larger culture. The result is an international imbalance in both support and appreciation for art, for music and for many other forms of creative expression.

Fierce Listeners understand that there is great benefit to righting this imbalance. One place to start is at the non-verbal, feeling level of personal exploration and expression.

Practice: *Notice how much of your daily life is involved with STEM activities. What might you do to bring considerable balance to both your work and your personal life? Who immediately comes to mind when you consider an ally who might be able to help right this imbalance?*

34. Improve Sensory Awareness by 1%

Our five senses mostly serve as filters of our experience. The things we see, hear, taste, smell and touch are taken in through receptors in each of the responsible sensory organs and transmitted to the brain as digital data - 1s or 0s - electrical impulses that sequence on or off pulsations.

Because our experiences seem so rich and full, it never occurs to us that any data might have been lost or filtered during transmission. But cybernetic research and information science has determined without a doubt that it absolutely has. How much? Get this - as much as 99% of what's possible to fully apprehend never makes it to conscious awareness.[25]

So, what this means is that roughly 1% of the sensory data - the sights, sounds, tastes, smells and things we touch - is only what each of us normally walks through the world consciously taking in.

But, what if we were to double our sensory capacity ... to 2%? Might you, as a Fierce Listener develop creative ways to facilitate that for people?

Practice: *Slow down and experiment with your senses. The next conversation you find yourself engaged in, imagine that there is far more to hear than you customarily are able to. Things you might ordinarily not hear you might find being expressed in voice tone, or speech rhythm, or in body language. Or, even in the things people are making conscious or unconscious decisions not to give voice to. Can you clearly hear what's not being said?*

35. Become a Safe Container for Secrets

Keeping secrets is bad for the brain. We know from research by James Pennebaker[26] and other psychologists that people who hold guilty or shameful secrets inside and never let them out essentially validates the wisdom teaching: " If you bring forth what is within you, what you bring forth will save you. If you do not bring forth what is within you, what you do not bring forth will kill you."

Making it safe for people to surface and disclose secrets is a central tenet of Fierce Listening. In order to do so, most people need first of all to feel psychologically and emotionally safe. They need to be certain that their confession will not be met with judgment or criticism or that it will in some way rupture or adversely affect the relationship. This can be a tall order for us engaged in a Fierce Listening practice, especially when the thing someone confesses may violate a strong moral principle that we hold.

Practice: *What makes it safe for you to disclose guilty or shameful secrets to another person? How does your body feel while you're holding such a secret inside? How does it feel after you have had the opportunity to fully express this withheld confession?*

36. Expand the Harmony Window to Remain Safely Between Rigidity and Chaos

In recent years sensorimotor psychotherapists[27] have introduced the concept of "the window of arousal" into common consciousness. Essentially what that means is that most of us operate in our daily lives within a certain harmonic range of emotional comfort. For some of us that range is pretty deep and wide. For others, it feels shallow and narrow.

All of us exceed that range from time to time. Excess on the low end takes us into areas where we feel despondent, depressed or quite limited or rigid in our thinking and actions; excess on the high end often finds us being anxious, hyper-alert, confused and operating on the edge of chaos.

A primary perspective from a Fierce listening standpoint is to be curious about skillful ways to help people close windows that are open too wide, and open windows that not open enough.

Practice: *Do you generally fall on the high end or the low end of the Harmony window? What tends to help bring you back into balance during those times when life circumstances move you in one direction or the other? How might you* *expand the "righting" resources you are able to bring to bear during those times?*

37. Listen with the Heart in Mind

Most of us don't realize that the heart has neurons just like the brain does (all the hollow organs do, in fact). Much as they do in the brain, these cells process energy and information - they constantly communicate the state of the body to the brain and receive "instruction sets" back from the brain.

While little official scientific research considers the heart to be the center of intelligence in terms of energy and information flow in human beings, more and more interest is being privately funded to accurately assess its role in optimal human functioning.

But regardless of what science determines, most of us can readily identify and appreciate people we consider to have "great heart." And Fierce Listening can be used to help cultivate that quality in others. How? In lots of creative ways.

One way might simply be to ask, "How might a person of Great Heart operate in these circumstances?" Another: "What needs to happen in order for you to grow strength of heart?"

Practice: *Consider the strength of your own heart. What people, places or circumstances tend to test its strength? What might you need to take on as a personal "heart-strengthening" practice? Who might you enlist to help you in these efforts?*

38. Don't Let the Snake Fly the Plane

The human brain has evolved into three major parts: the neocortex, the limbic system and the reptilian complex. Letting the snake fly the plane refers to those times when we "close down the thinker," throw reason and caution to the winds and find ourselves flooded with the reactive stress hormones, adrenaline and cortisol. Few good things happen as a consequence of letting our stressed selves run operations.

The Golden Rule of Social Neuroscience operates on the realization that it takes "a more organized brain to help organize a less organized brain." This is ideally the process by which parents, teachers, clergy, counselors and Fierce Listeners help others grow and internalize their own ability to self-monitor and emotionally self-regulate. But until that capacity is firmly in place and able to operate easily amidst a wide variety of situations and circumstances, we can place our capacity for deep listening in service to that growth.

Practice: *Spend some time in the coming days paying attention to those fear or anxiety-driven times when you and others end up with the snake at the controls of your life. What tools do you currently have at your disposal that might work to take back control from the snake and bring something Buddhists call "Brilliant Sanity" to bear?*

39. Recognize that You're a Pleasure to Talk To

Talkers populate the world. They assume that someone is listening, even though extensive testing has determined that only a small portion of anything people say gets retained and integrated by listeners in kind of meaningful manner.

To encounter someone who not only knows the value and power inherent in listening to others for both speaker and listener, and someone who has genuinely and willingly taken this endeavor on as a personal pursuit, is to find a very precious gem of a person, indeed. As such, determine to hold your gift in its proper place in your life, rejoicing in whatever benefits you are gracefully able to bring to the hearts, minds, bodies and souls of others. The best benefits are almost always mutual.

Practice: *Give some contemplative thought to just how useful and valuable someone dedicated to the practice of Fierce Listening truly is in a world which so values speech. As an exercise in humble self-appreciation, see if you can get in touch with what a blessing the fact that you have taken up this practice truly is to yourself and other beings.*

Section Three Reflection Questions

What does it feel like when I listen deeply to someone?

What have I heard recently that I may have found disturbing or confounding? How did I respond?

What have I noticed about my capacity to pay ever closer, non-distracted attention?

Notes to myself...

"Listening is an attitude of the heart, a genuine desire to be with another which both attracts and heals."
~ Sura Hart

"Love is the very difficult understanding that something other than yourself is real."
~ Iris Murdock

"A Spectacle of Silence."

I once witnessed a spectacle of silence in the Berkeley Community Theater. Every one of the 3,491 seats was occupied. On stage sat a Buddhist monk. Next to him sat a young woman. The monk spoke about mindfulness, about awareness, about respect for each other and all living things. He spoke slowly and quietly. From time to time he would fall silent, and the woman would pick up and ring a bell that rested on the floor in front of her. The reverberations of the bell could be heard throughout the auditorium and felt within each person's brain, stimulating perceptions of intuitive subtlety.

The talk was less about information than experience. The words were like a tour bus carrying the audience to ancient sites of meaning and depth and beauty. Though the bus was still and unmoving, we traveled far and saw much. Anyone could have dropped a tack or a nail file, even a piece of paper, and the noise would have seemed loud because the silence was so great.

After some time, I felt the audience breathe in unison, a meditative breathing, a breathing that connected us together and to the awareness of which the monk was speaking. I thought I was sitting in the mountains at twilight, when life itself begins to creep from its hiding places like a deer come to drink from a lake of pentagrams and stars.

Even when speaking, the monk was silent, was silence. In order to hear his words of silence and the silence within his words, the audience had to be silent and become silence. It was a spectacle. We were embraced by silence and thus set free from agitation, from separation, from duality. It would have been impossible for any anger or cruelty to arise in that community. It would have been impossible for anyone to harm another in any way. We were transported to reality.

Silence cannot be explained. It cannot be known or experienced in a way that might be familiar to us, as we are used to experiencing other events in our life. However, when we say beauty or love, and when we are meeting those two in a pure and honest place, then we can say that silence has come into our life.

We can only use words to point in the direction of silence, such that if one actually goes into the distance towards which the words point, one will eventually come upon silence as a fact. When silence is beheld as a fact, all speculation, argument, and belief about that to which the word silence refers ends instantly and forever.

Silence is that in which everything exists, from which everything comes, and into which everything returns. It is the unutterable context in which the cosmos occurs, a playground of pure consciousness.

Silence is oneness. Silence refers to a state of fundamental unified existence, a condition of being in which all conflict, fear, doubt, projection, memory, delusions - all subjectivity and objectivity - are dissolved and thus resolved. Silence is an instantaneous recognition of that which is out of time and unconditioned by cause and effect. If one were a religious person, one could say that silence is the soul of God, or perhaps the God of God.

If this sounds abstract, vague, or esoteric, it only sounds so because we cannot say exactly what silence is. Some things are so very beyond the reach of words and metaphors, symbols and images, beliefs and concepts that all attempts to describe them are foolish.

And yet, even as we speak foolishly and impertinently of that which cannot be said, something within us will smile knowingly. It is this intuitive resonance which words can stimulate. This is the direction we can point to and go toward, walking or running, in order for the recognition of the wordless to become real. But even as silence becomes indomitably real, as taut and tense and thrilling as a tidal wave crashing upon us, crushing us beyond recognition - even as this happens, we cannot speak its truth.

Any disciplined practice that involves focusing the mind will eventually lead to silence. Spiritual methods such as meditation techniques, chanting mantras, yoga, tai chi - all of these will lead to silence. Self-inquiry will lead to silence. So will martial arts, and dance, and art. So will rock climbing and sky-diving. So will cooking and eating. So will playing and loving. Everything will lead to silence, because silence is the life force behind everything. It is the oxygen without which everything would fall over dead, flash frozen. Since all things lead to silence, we must follow the echoes of silence, inward, to the source of all things within us.

Being led to silence might imply that silence is somewhere else. This is only a figure of speech. Silence is always the first thing and the last thing. It is always present, but very subtle, so we must therefore learn to recognize it. The direction of silence is any direction. There is no place that silence is not, although we cannot apprehend it with our senses or with our minds.

Still, let me suggest a foolproof way of coming into silence quickly, so that silence becomes a fact for us. First, we must develop the ability to distinguish one thought from another. When we can do this, we must then develop the ability to see clearly the space between two thoughts. When that space becomes large and stable enough for us to drive a truck through it, we will know silence as a fact.

In the very center of universal manifestation, one finds swirling gusts of silence, vast galactic streamers millions of light years long. If we try to understand this silence through our mind, we'll never understand it. Silence is realized in a moment of communion, in a moment of losing our separation from life. The underlying truth of existence is silence. Silence embraces everything and cannot be known because to know silence, we would have to be separate from silence, and silence would then be an object of our perception and of our knowing. Silence refers to that which is beyond this dualism of knower and known. Silence becomes a fact when we and life become an inseparable whole.

Even though we are trying to define it, no definition of silence is accurate. We don't want to think that by defining it, we can know it.

Silence is knowable only to itself, and we come into that knowing through an alchemy of self-transcendence. We can only create a definition that points to silence. The truth of reality is silent. It is undisturbed. It is causeless. It is out of time, out of space, non-dual. Silence is the preeminent nothingness in which the universe dances in spectacular and mysterious ways.

If silence is the United States, then intuition is Ellis Island, the first stop of immigrants seeking asylum. Intuition is the first hint, the first experience of the far greater country of silence. Intuition is not a tool, but rather an intelligence that uses us. We might not see this right away. Intuition is willing to be used, but only for a time. One day, it will require that we suspend our goals and objectives, our plans and aspirations, for a fuller recognition of what intuition is, what it represents. We will come to see that intuition is the ambassador of silence, and we must serve that silence, for it is the soul of the world.

In the instant of intuitive perception, we are taken wholly into that power of knowing which is beyond the mind. In going beyond the mind, we go beyond all notions of self and identity, of thought and belief, of perceiver and perceived. A photograph of the intuitive flash would show only light. There would be no other image, only light. The light of intuition is the light of consciousness. Intuition is Ellis Island, the gateway to freedom. In order to be free, we must want freedom, we must be willing to leave behind the old countries of control and manipulation from which we have come. We cannot come to this new country with ideas of exploitation, as gangsters. We have to come as servants of the new freedom. We have to learn new ways of living. We have to become students of silence and freedom in order to learn how to live without fear, without violence, without cruelty.

~ adapted from Robert Rabbin
Echoes of Silence

40. Enrich Contingent Communication

Scientists who study human development and emotional and psychological attachment have identified one essential interaction that profoundly contributes to both those processes in human beings. They have named that interaction ... contingent communication.

Contingent communication is manna for brain development – not only in children – but all across the lifespan. What exactly is it and why will we wither without it?

There are essentially 3 elements, all of which involve Fierce Listening. The first is we need to be paying attention. We need to be able to recognize that something is being communicated to us in all its nuance and complexity.

Oftentimes, this is not so easy or obvious. Great shades of subtlety can be involved, including what's NOT being communicated – those things that "go without saying."

Once we've given over our attention, we need to be able to make appropriate and accurate meaning of the message being sent. If a baby's crying, we change her diaper, attempt to feed her, rock her or sing her a lullaby. If she continues to cry, we haven't accurately received and understood the message. This need for being accurately understood - for "feeling felt" -

continues throughout the lifespan. How that understanding gets communicated back to us (and I consider this a great modern-day challenge) is by being responded to in a *timely* and *effective* manner – the third and final critical element of contingent communication.

Think about how much of the communication in the world today – from movies, TV and radio, to advertising and email spam, to preachers and teachers preaching and teaching at us. Even this book – to the extent that I send it out to the many and only hear back and exchange ideas with a few – falls into the category of non-contingent communication.

Practice: *Look around you. Pay close attention to all the needs, wishes and wants you put out into the world on a regular basis that receive little or no response in return. Resolve to improve your own capacity for contingent responsiveness.*

41. Listen Without Intent to Do Good

The most skillful Fierce Listening is simply done for listening's sake with nothing added. There is no desire to "help," no socially or personally prescribed winning behavior. It is not done in order for us to feel good about ourselves or to reinforce the "syndrome of the server." It is simply listening for listening's sake. But what if we find ourselves adding things on to our listening? What if indeed, we are trying to offer something we think of as beneficial for ourselves and others? Afterall, there is a growing body of research evidence[2] that suggests that listeners benefit even more than speakers from listening.

When you find yourself listening in order to get or give something, a skillful response would be to simply observe this desire, be with it, and then do your best to relax, let it go and ... just listen.

Practice: Pay increasing attention to thoughts and desires that may arise in your listening practice that may compromise your ability to be fully present, just listening. Often they will show up as some sort of pain or tension in your own body. Pay further attention to that pain or tension and see what thoughts or feelings might spontaneously pop into your head that may or may not be connected.

42. Practice Listening to Regulate the Body

Stanford neuroscientist Karl Pribram has identified that one of the primary purposes of our brain is to regulate physical and emotional arousal.[28] To the extent it functions as a contemplative practice, Fierce Listening can be a superb means of providing the brain with an effective "assist" in the regulation department.

Not only does listening allow us to flex and strengthen our "presence muscles," but it also allows us to monitor and adjust our own levels of arousal. As a by-product of that adjustment, due to our resonance circuitry and the "contagion effect" we are also able to positively affect the arousal levels of the people around us. Fierce Listening then becomes a vehicle for attaining the exalted state that Rudyard Kipling referenced in his famous poem, "If." - "If you can keep your head when all about you are losing theirs and blaming it on you ..."

Practice: *Begin noticing the effect on breathing and heart rate that your own listening practice has on you. Can you simultaneously sense that a similar effect gets transmitted to the people in your immediate presence? Some research shows that the extended range of the electromagnetic field of our heart extends out in as much as an 8 foot radius! Do you think it matters whether or not that heart is tranquil or agitated? Do you think it matters whether the effect is conscious or unconscious?*

43. Activate Your Dalai Lama Neurons

In his book, *The Tell-Tale Brain*[29], noted University of California neuroscientist V. S. Ramachandran identifies certain neural connections in our brain as being necessary and sufficient for being able to feel and express empathy in the world. He termed these "Dalai Lama Neurons." These brain cells are sometimes also called mirror neurons. Their connections are formed during a critical period when the developmental window in children for establishing something research neuroscientists call Theory of Mind is formed.

But what if development goes awry and someone is not afforded sufficient opportunity to grow and make these brain connections? Brain plasticity, it turns out, allows for them to be formed all through the lifespan. And the practice and presentation of Fierce Listening can play a central role in that subsequent neural unfolding. When we practice and model empathy and connection for those who have not fully developed those capacities in themselves, Dalai Lama Neurons have a chance to grow through a process called neurogenesis and then make new connections through a complementary process called synaptogenesis. Fierce Listening is very good for your brain and for everyone else's!

Practice: *Just for fun, see if you can imagine or pretend that you are able to feel new cells forming and making new connections in your own brain. It happens all the time, moment after moment, whether we're aware of it or not. New cells making new connections lies at the very foundation of all life.*

44. Listen for the Loose Brick

One of the foundational teachings of Non-Violent Communication is that we all have needs. And when those needs are great and they don't get met, communication tends to go wonky.

A creative lens to listen through in order to suss out needs that people have that they may not be aware of, is to "listen for the loose brick."

Rather than "batting your head against a brick wall," listening for the loose brick is an orientation that looks for the unmet need that, once met, will dismantle the brick wall with little further effort.

Very often those needs are quite simple: the need to be validated; to be respected; to be fully understood; to feel connected; to have our intentions accurately reflected back to us; to feel genuinely felt, mostly at the emotional level. The result often ends up that we feel deeply appreciated and cared for.

Practice: Do a personal inventory and identify the people in your life who are especially adept at recognizing and reflecting back the places in you where loose bricks live. What is it about them that you most value? If you don't have too many people like that around you, what might it take to gather more?

45. Clear Your Emotional Cache

In computer technology, the cache is the place where the machine stores memories, operating instructions that it can readily access to perform the same behaviors over and over.

For a Fierce Listener, clearing our own memory stores is an effective way to enter into dialogue as unbiased a mindset as possible. It also can serve as an emotional cleansing procedure, allowing us to come with a fresh perspective and something akin to Beginner's Heart.

Learning to come to people, places and situations with a clear perspective honors the process of growth and change that is unfolding in each of us constantly, even though, for the most part we are unaware of it.

Practice: *Begin paying some attention to the feelings that arise, peak and then subside as we interact with any number of people in the days of our lives. How challenging is it to simply "be with" and observe these feelings and not be reactive in response to them? Do you think it might be possible to never be "tossed away" by our afflictive emotions?*

46. Listen for the Purpose of Hacking Flow

In his detailed account of how performance is being surpassed across a broad number of human endeavors, research journalist Steve Kotler provides us with 10 activities that correlate closely with individuals' and organizations who are regularly able to "hack" what psychologist Mihalyi Csikszentmihalyi[30] identified in the 1970s as the peak performance "flow state." Fierce Listening, it turns out plays a key role.

Here are the other nine triggers Kotler identifies in his book, *The Rise of Superman*[12]:

    1. Serious concentration
    2. Shared, clear goals
    3. Communication with lots of feedback
    4. Equal participation
    5. Elements of risk
    6. Familiarity and trust

7. Blending egos
8. Sense of control
9. Additive interactions

This last element simply means that interactions are designed to build momentum, togetherness and innovation as a means of perpetually amplifying one another's ideas and actions.

***Practice:** Give some thought to how you might want to both practice and surround yourself with others who are also committed to the possibility of dedicating some time and energy in their lives to the pursuit of learning how to access flow states on a regular basis. How do you imagine the time spent with such people might positively impact your life? Might there also be a negative downside?*

47. Make Meaning of Silence

Stanford professor Susan Dunn contends that silence is a most meaningful experience around sound. It's important when we listen in our relationships, that we listen to what is said, and also to what is not said. It's important that we especially listen to the silences that punctuate our conversations. Here are ten perspectives on silence that a Fierce Listener would be wise to be mindful of.

1. Silence is not the same as soundlessness, or the absence of sound. Silence is to sound as sleep is to life. Silence very often is full of meaning. With some silences you want to say - Let's talk about what we're not talking about, or Lets be silent about something else. Some silences are so full of the thing that neither is able to deal with verbally at the moment you can almost reach out and touch it.

2. There's a sullen, hostile silence that literally pulses with struggle. When someone's afraid to express their anger or disappointment, or is determined to make the other person take control and do something.

3. There's a silence that is just quietly being with someone else. Sometimes we're with someone and each gets intent on their own project. We're so comfortable with that person that we don't need to fill the air with words. That's a very comfortable feeling. Between two people silence can be a place where a person can simply be, can simply live along, without making any effort to communicate or focus. There is a mutual sense of the space, a natural space of being.

4. There's the long, heavy silence of embarrassment or shame. Our emotions tell

us things we need to know about what's going on. Sometimes we realize we've done something we wish we hadn't and feel embarrassment or shame. This feeling tells us we need to change something so we can feel good about ourselves again.

5. Silence can be a receptive position where our whole being is open to the unspoken messages from the other. When we're really open to listening to the other person, they'll know it.

6. Silence allows a space for contemplation. Sometimes someone says something to us that really hits home. We need to take a moment, or longer, to let it sink in, to think about what's been said and to process the feelings.

7. There is the silence of awe - when something is too wonderful or too awful to be commented upon. When we listen to a tragic story, or hear of a synchronous wonderful event, the appropriate response is often silence. When we listen to a mother describing her baby, or a woman describing the man she loves, or an old person talking about their dreams and memories, or a father talking of his son who has died we sometimes don't know what to say and our emotional response is a profound silence that is full of emotion.

8. Silence can express our most alert attending. There's an alert, crackling kind of silence, such as when we're taking in some intellectual piece of information and are struggling to hear and to understand every part of it. We're excited and paying close attention and all ears.

9. Under all speech that is good for anything, there lies a silence that is better. Silence is deep as Eternity; speech is shallow as Time. There are times that are so profound we just don't have words, but the position of our silence can allow a meeting place with the other that's very meaningful. Words fail us at times, because they just aren't adequate to express what we're feeling.

10. Silence is a dynamic no man's land shared equally by speaker and listener, belonging to neither and yet to both. Silence can be a very special place between two can begin to skillfully listen to ourselves as we listen more skillfully to others.

Practice: *Determine to spend recurring and increasing amounts of time paying attention to the silence within which speech unfolds. How does the focus on the "negative space" of speech change both the content, context and meaning of what you actually hear?*

48. Listen to Grow the 8 Intelligences

In 1983 Harvard education professor, Howard Gardner[31] first proposed his theory of multiple intelligences. Here's what he originally had to say about them:

> Multiple intelligences is a psychological theory about the mind. It's a critique of the notion that there's a single intelligence which we're born with, which can't be changed, and which psychologists can measure. It's based on a lot of scientific research in fields ranging from psychology to anthropology to biology. It's not based upon test correlations, which most other intelligence theories are based on. The claim is that there are at least eight different human intelligences. Most intelligence tests look at language or logic or both - those are just two of the intelligences. The other six are musical, spatial, bodily/kinesthetic, interpersonal, intrapersonal, and naturalist. I make two claims. The first claim is that all human beings have all of these intelligences. It's part of our species definition. The second claim is that, both because of our genetics and our environment, no two people have

exactly the same profile of intelligences, not even identical twins, because their experiences are different.

Fierce Listeners not only have a conscious awareness of these eight intelligences, but they also do whatever they can to help others facilitate their internal unfolding in ways that are specific and distinctive to each person as a prized and unique individual. Essentially, they work to help themselves and each other bring as many intelligences as possible to fullest flower.

49. Ask Quality Questions

Quality questions expand thinking, create engagement, and encourage people to apply ideas to real life. Here are some sample questions that illustrate these principles:

What life work might hold the greatest heart and meaning for me?

What steps might I complete that would enable me to begin doing it?

What obstacles stand in the way? What might be creative, effective ways around them?

Who might I be able to enlist to help me in the performance of this life work?

Practice: *Give some thought to what growth and change in your own current personal circumstances might look like. Come up with a dozen or so Quality Questions that might help clarify what direction that change and growth might require you to move in.*

50. Transform the Dark into the Light

After many years of working with people as a neuropsychologist, Diana Fosha has come to the inescapable conclusion that "people have a fundamental need for transformation. We are wired for growth, healing, and self-righting, that is, to resume impeded growth."[32]

One form that healing might take is deliberately surfacing traumatic memories from earlier times in our lives - the Dark - and finding creative ways to both verbally give voice to them and move our bodies in ways we were not able to at the time those memories got laid down.

Fierce Listeners understand how memories become laid down in the brain and end up removed from conscious awareness. They also understand the value in providing a safe place for such expression to take place in ways that ultimately lead to healing, integrative, multi-sensory resolution.

Practice: *Find a willing confederate whom you trust and begin exploring some of your own earliest overwhelming experiences. Notice whatever might arise to inhibit their full expression. At the same time, be aware of all the ways that your body was restricted at the time of those experiences. Also, be aware of the importance of being able to freely move your body in response to resurfacing those memories.*

51. Listen for Momento Mori

Programmed deep into the cells of our body and brain is the awareness that one day we will all die. This natural process - apoptosis - goes on at the cellular level in every moment of our lives. This unconscious awareness informs much of the way that we engage with life, inviting us to turn towards or to turn away from many opportunities that life presents.

The ancient Romans had a phrase for the process of bringing death to conscious awareness. That phrase is *momento mori* - remember death. Providing support for people who wish to reflect on mortality can become a vehicle for embracing the transient nature of all earthly life and material pursuits. It can be a way to place death awareness into service for living a deepened, meaningful life. Very often what that life turns out to be is a life of service.

Practice: *Give some consideration to the reality of your own eventual death. If you were to imagine your life at its end, what might you want to look back on and feel little regret over? What might you want to take great pride in having engaged in and devoted much of your life's time and energy to? Is there currently a need to course-correct?*

52. Model and Engage in The Protégé Effect

The Roman philosopher, Seneca said, "While we teach, we learn." Contemporary brain research has published a number of studies that show how repeating something we wish to learn and remember so as to be able to make good use of it, works most consistently when we attach feelings to the learning. Teaching can certainly make us feel all sorts of things.

In accord with that notion is a study[33] by one of my favorite researchers, Annie Murphy Paul. What she found is that people who teach others what they are trying to learn themselves, far surpass those who only do the learning directly.

Teaching others Fierce Listening forces us to not only organize and present the material in interesting, dynamic ways that might creatively engage a learner, but it also requires us to reflect on notions and concepts we might not be totally clear about and then go deeper in order to solidify our understanding.

Practice: *Find a willing "victim" and make good use of The Protégé Effect by offering to teach or coach them in applying any number of the practices in this little book. You might begin teaching the ones that you feel like you might not have the strongest grasp of yourself.*

Section Four Reflection Questions

Which areas of my life have been positively transformed by practicing the skills in this book?

Whom do I think might benefit from receiving a copy of this book?

Who can I ask to join me in a Community of Practice in learning to be a more skilled listener?

Notes to myself...

Conclusion

Fierce Listening is without a doubt a challenging practice. In my own work I get it "wrong" way more often than I get it right, based upon the knowledge I have and the standards I have set for myself. In that regard, I'm like a skillful baseball player: I can bat .333 and still end up being enshrined in the Listening Hall of Fame!

When it comes right down to it though, *Fierce Listening* is a lot like meditation practice. In fact, it can be a form of meditation: every time I notice I have stopped skillfully listening, I simply pause, gather my sensory resources and do my best to fully attend once again. Here's to you adding yourself to the growing number of people committed to transforming the world through the power of an open ear and heart.

References

1. Brady, Mark (2015). *Noble listening.* Langley, WA: Paideia Press.

2. Schwartz, Carolyn & Sendor, Meir (1999). Helping others helps oneself: Response shift in peer support. *Social Science & Medicine*, 48, No. 11, 1563-1575.

3. Porges, Stephen (2011). *The polyvagal theory: Neurophysiological foundations of emotions, attachment, communication, and self-regulation.* NY: W.W. Norton.

4. Maurer, Robert (2014). *One small step can change your life: The kaizen way.* NY: Workman Publishing.

5. Levitin, Daniel J. (2014). *The organized mind.* NY: Dutton.

6. Mattis-Namgyel, Elizabeth (2010). *The power of an Open Question.* Boston: Shambhala Publications.

7. Menon, Vinod & Uddin, L.Q. (2010). Saliency, switching, attention and control: A

network model of insula function. in *Brain Structure and Function*. NY: Springer.

8. Grice, Paul (1991). *Studies in the ways of words.* Cambridge, MA: Harvard University Press.

8. Seung, Sebastian (2012). *Connectome: How the brain makes us who we are.* NY: Houghton Mifflin Harcourt.

9. Murphy-Paul, Annie (2012). Your brain on fiction. *New York Times*. March 18, pg. SR6.

10. Boulenger, Véronique (2010). Interwoven functionality in the brain's action and language system. *The Mental Lexicon*, 231-254.

11. Jarvis, Debra (2014). Yes, I survived cancer. But that doesn't define me. *TED Talk.* http://bit.ly/1E3u3Ic

12. Kotler, Steve (2014). *The rise of superman: Decoding the science of ultimate human performance.* NY: New Harvest.

13. Batty-Herbert, Kimberley (1999). *The Dolittle Method of Listening.* International Listening Association. http://d1025403.site.

myhosting.com/files.listen.org/Swap%20Shop/Swap_Shop_1999.pdf

14. Mate, Gabor. (2010). *In the realm of hungry ghosts.* Berkeley, CA: North Atlantic Books.

15. Sapolsky, Robert (2004). *Why zebras don't get ulcers.* NY: Henry Holt and Company.

16. Mellon, Nancy (2008). *Body eloquence.* Santa Rosa, CA: Energy Psychology Press.

17. Elaine Reese, Catherine A. Haden, Lynne Baker-Ward, Patricia Bauer, Robyn Fivush, and Peter A. Ornstein (2011). Coherence of personal narratives across the lifespan: A multidimen-sional model and coding method. *Journal of Cognitive Development, Oct-Dec; 12(4): 424–462.*

18. Iacoboni, Marco (2009). *Mirroring people: The science of empathy and how we connect with others.* NY: Picador.

19. Rizzolati, Giacomo (2008). *Mirrors in the brain: How our minds share actions, emotions, and experience.* London: Oxford University Press.

20. Kahneman, Daniel (2011). *Thinking, fast and slow.* NY: Farrar, Straus and Giroux.

21. Bolas, Christopher (2011). *The Christopher Bolas reader.* London: Routledge.

22. Porges, Stephen (2013). *Dharma Cafe interview with William Stranger.* May 15, https://www.youtube.com/watch?v=8tz146HQotY

23. Jones, J.T., Pelham, B.W., Carvallo, M., and Mirenberg, M.C. (2004). How do I love thee? Let me count the Js: Implicit egotism and interpersonal attraction. *Journal of Personality and Social Psychology*, 87 (5): 665-683.

24. Eagleman, David (2011). *Incognito: The secret lives of the brain.* NY: Pantheon.

25. Zimmerman, M. (1989). The nervous system in the context of information theory. In *Human Physiology,* Schmidt & Thews, Editors. Berlin: Springer-Verlag.

26. Pennebaker, James (1985). Traumatic experience and psychosomatic disease: Exploring the roles of behavioral inhibition, obsession and confiding. *Canadian Psychology*, 26: 82-95.

27. Ogden, P., Minton, K. and Pain, C. (2006). *Trauma and the body: A sensorimotor approach to psychotherapy*. NY: W. W. Norton.

28. Pribram, Karl (2013). *The form within: My point of view.* NY: Prospecta Press.

29. Ramachandran, V. S. (2012). *The tell-tale brain: A neuroscientist's quest for what makes us human.* NY: W. W. Norton.

30. Csikszentmihalyi, Mihalyi (2013). *Creativity: The psychology of discovery and invention.* NY: Harper.

31. Gardner, Howard (1983). *Frames of mind: The theory of multiple intelligences.* NY: Basic Books.

32. Fosha, Diana, Siegel, Daniel, & Solomon, Marion (Eds.) (2009). *The Healing Power of Emotion: Affective Neuroscience, Development & Clinical Practice.* NY: W. W. Norton.

33. Murphy-Paul, Annie (2011). The protégé effect. On the blog, *Brilliant.* Nov. 30, 2011. http://ideas.time.com/2011/11/30/the-protege-effect/

34. Sullivan, Bob and Thompson, Hugh. (2013). Now hear this: Most people stink at listening. *Scientific American Online*, Mar. 3. http://www. scientificamerican.com/article/plateau-effect-digital-gadget-distraction-attention/

Listening Skills Bibliography

Adler, Mortimer (1983). *How to Speak; How to Listen.* New York: Simon and Schuster.

Brady, Mark (Ed.) (2003). *The Wisdom of Listening.* Somerville, MA: Wisdom Publications.

Burley-Allen, Madelyn (1995). *Listening : The Forgotten Skill (A Self-Teaching Guide).* NY: John Wiley & Son.

Ghoulston, Mark (2010). *Just listen.* NY: Amacom Publishing.

Lindahl, Kay (2003). *Practicing the Sacred Art of Listening.* Woodstock, VT: Skylight Paths Publishing.

Nichols, Michael P. (1995). *The Lost Art of Listening.* New York: The Guilford Press.

Patterson, K., Grenny, J., McMillan, R. & Switzler, A. (2002). *Crucial Conversations.* NY: McGraw-Hill.

Purdy, M & Ridge, P. (2000). *Listening Bibliography.* http://www.listen.org/Bib

Rosenberg, Marshall B. (2003). *Nonviolent Communication: A Language of Life.* Encinitas, CA: Puddledancer Press.

Shafir, Rebecca Z. (2000). *The Zen of Listening: Mindful Communication in the Age of Distraction.* Wheaton, IL: Quest Books.

Steil, Lyman and Bommelje, Rick (2004*). Listening Leaders.* Edina, MN: Beaver's Pond Press, Inc.

About the Author:

Mark Brady is an award-winning author, teacher, and trainer. He has taught graduate courses in skillful listening for the last dozen years. He has edited the listening anthology, *The Wisdom of Listening* and written numerous articles for journals and national magazines. He is the prize-winning author of a number of books. The most recent is entitled *A Father's Book of Listening*. It and the others can be ordered from bookstores or on the Internet or by emailing: paideia@gmail.com.

Contact us

We hope you enjoyed this book and the transformations taking place in your life as you've practiced some of the skills. We invite you to send us your comments, ideas and any stories you'd like to share at the addresses below. We'd be delighted to hear from you!

To contact Mark Brady for more information:
Email: doctormarkbrady@gmail.com
P.O. Box 1294
Langley, WA 98260
Office: (206) 201-2212

To Order:

To order copies of *Fierce Listening* send a check for $16.95 (includes shipping and handling) to:

Paideia Press,
P.O. Box 1294,
Langley, WA 98260

(WA residents send $17.95 which includes tax and shipping.) Please remember to include your shipping information. Orders of 20 or more copies are discounted. Please contact us for pricing and shipping information.